Want To Make The World A Better Place?

Want To Make The World A Better Place?

Hayden Harshman

Nectar Publications
Savannah, Geogia

Want To Make The World A Better Place

Copyright © 2021 by Hayden Harshman
Illustrations by Mary Sullivan
Edited by Lindsey Grovenstein

This book was typeset in Campanile and Adobe Garamond Pro.

All rights reserved. This is the work of fiction. Names, characters, places, and incidents are either the product of the author's imagination or, if real, are used fictitiously. No part of this book may be used or reproduced, transmitted, or stored in any manner whatsoever by any means, graphic, electronic, or mechanical, including photocopying, taping, and recording, without written permission except in the case of brief quotations embodied in critical articles and reviews. For more information, please contact the author, illustrator, or publisher, Nectar Publications.

First edition 2021

(Paperback) ISBN: 978-0-9859986-4-6
(Ebook) ISBN: 978-0-9859986-7-7

Nectar Publications, LLC
P.O. Box 6552
Savannah, Georgia 31414
visit us at www.nectarpublications.com

Printed in the United States of America

Intro

In my early twenties, my intuition was cluing me to change my diet. I became curious about why human teeth are flat and why animal teeth are pointed. Many questions and research lead me to what the effects of meat-eating are on the body and the environment. Feeling compassion and empathy toward the world and listening to that gut feeling, I quit. Mid sandwich. Cold turkey, hot turkey, chicken, red meats, and all other animals.

I assembled and "trans-rhyme-scribed" (transcribed into rhymes) what I thought would be an entertaining and enlightening read of compiled research from various perspectives on how we can make ourselves and the world a better us and place.

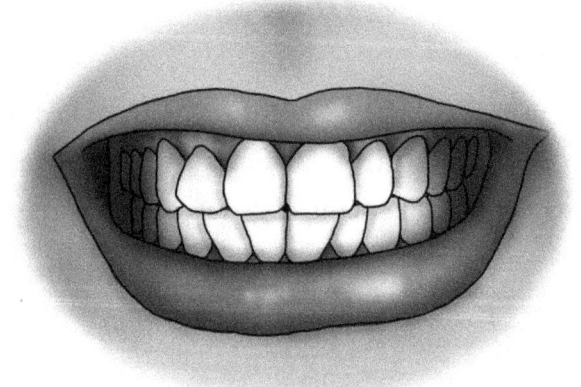

First

Study your teeth. It's what started it for me. Carnivores have fangs for shredding the meat. Herbivores have flat teeth for chewing on leaves, seeds, fruits, and veggies.

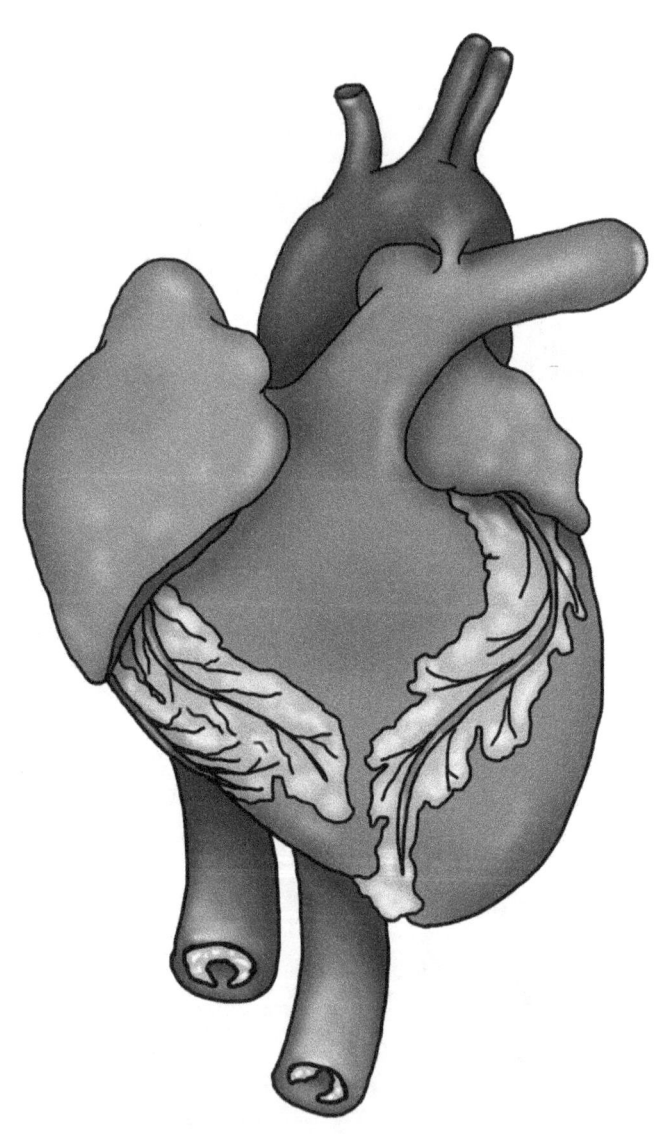

Secondly

Almost instantly, upon death, meat purifies. Served fresh
with poisonous effects.
It's why carnivores have small intestinal tracts to digest.
As for humans, the intestinal tract is twelve times the length of the
body. Flesh remains and begins rotting,
creating free radicals, destructive oxygen atoms causing cancer.
Severely damageable.
It requires a large amount
of hydrochloric acid to break meat down.
Humans produce less than one twentieth
of the acid produced by carnivores who can stomach it.
Humans prefer roast beast.
Cooking destroys the enzymes present in the meat
that aids in digesting the carnivore's feast.
A human's pancreas could cease if stressed,
weakened by producing more enzymes, inviting disease.
Over the years, when excess fats are consumed,
fatty deposits called plague build onto and clog the hearts tubes.
Hardening of the arteries. Constricting blood flow,
increasing the risk for blood clots, heart attack, and strokes.

Three

One of the thousands of drugs being pumped into the cow's blood is
RBGH/BST, a synthetic growth hormone causing disease,
to say the least, in the thyroid, breast, and bone,
transfers to humans. Fat cells are the hormone's home.
Bonded in the meat some eat and the milk some drink.
Chemicals used to preserve—to slow decay—give meat its red hue.
Its natural brown gray color turn people away.
A fine line between safe and dangerous.
From the blood of a corpse to human's blood,
these chemicals are contagious.

Four

Majority of crops are grown as cattle feed.
Corn, soy, cotton, and wheat
are permitted to have higher doses of pesticides—poisoning—
more so than crops sprayed for human beings.
Chemical residues are stored in fat tissues
that humans consume, not knowing the issues.

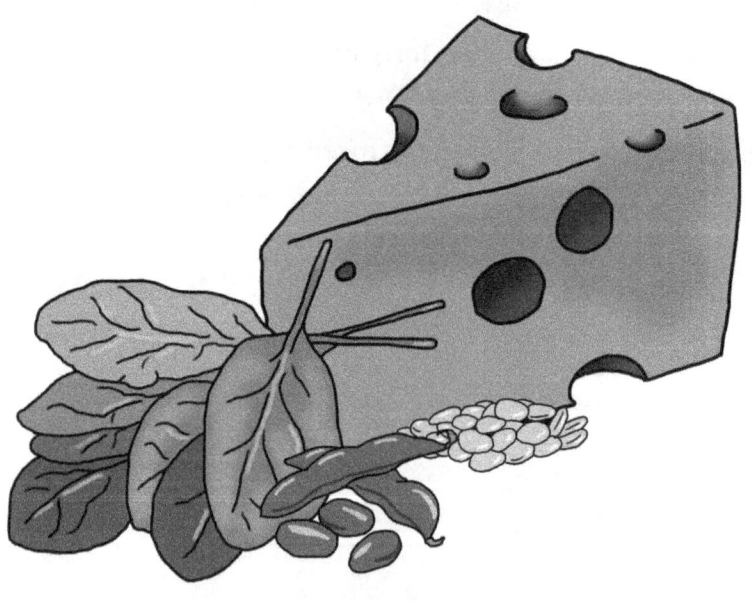

Five

We don't need large amounts of protein
for strength and energy. It's a myth.
Besides, 20 grams in three and a half ounces of meat
is less than the 25 in lentils or cheese.
An acre of beans or peas has ten times more protein
than an acre set aside for the production of meat.
We find 28 times
more protein in an acre of spinach leaves,
and 34 grams of protein in soybeans.
The true energy source is carbohydrates.
Our energy reduces with too much protein intake.

Six

16 pounds of grain produces one pound of beef. How many gallons of water are used? 5,214. 1,600 gallons of water for pork, 25 for wheat, 815 for a pound of chicken, and lettuce uses only 23.

Seven

Over 31 million cattle in the U.S are raised for beef.
Tainted manure and fertilizers runs off into the water we drink
near coastal areas, killing fish in the sea.
Factory farm fossil fuel fumes fill the air we breathe.
Nitrous oxide and methane gases
deoxygenate and warm the water, suffocating marine life in masses.
Illegally cutting down forests for pastures.
Destroying our natural carbon air filters
in exchange for cash and unnatural disasters.
Depleting the planet to satisfy the palate.

Eight

Tax dollars go to the meat industry.
Subsidized to survive with grants and favorable loan guarantees.
The government purchases their surplus,
which is often destroyed. Fiscally a wasteful purpose.

Nine

In terms of calorie units per acre,
a diet of grains, veggies, and beans
will support 20 times more people than a diet of meat.
If we primarily produced vegetarian foods
the planet could support 20 billion or more.
The Global Hunger Alliance writes,
"Most hunger deaths are due to chronic malnutrition,
caused by inequitable, or biased, distribution
and inefficient use of existing food resources."
Sometimes extra grain is thrown into the sea.
Some places profuse production and others are in scarcity.
Restrictions on the distribution of grain, due to
desire for profit and regulations on trade.
If there were a government to distribute grain
there would be no scarcity, no slaughter houses to maintain,
no need for false theories about overpopulation for personal gain.

Ten

A living cow provides more food than a dead one.
Butter, milk, cheese, and other foods in a continuous outcome.
That's why in most third world countries they keep the holy cow alive.
Cows eat grasses and harvested remains
like rice hulls and the tops of sugar cane.
The food problem has more to do with drought,
political upheaval, or industrialization than with cows.
In America, early 80's, the government stock piled
butter, dried milk, and cheese. 45 million pounds a week.
Millions of pounds were released to the poor and hungry for free.
Tragically, millions of dairy cows were bought and slaughtered
to end the need to support milk prices by stock piling dairy products.

Eleven

A cow produces ten times more food then a calf can consume.
Mother cow nurtures the children of humanity, too.
Father bull provides by tilling the land for crops and hauling lumber and sand,
cooperation with man.
Dung can be used for fuel after drying for cars, cooking, and lighting
and stirred in with their urine, given to plants to nourish.
Dung can be used in medicines,
treating disease caused by antibiotic resistant microorganisms.
The cow is mother earth manifest. When we mistreat her
nature's bounty withdraws and we are doomed for death.
Civilization ends. No more food resources left, what then?
She has been abused, neglected.
We are here to provide the earth with protection.
Oil wars for gas guzzling polluting machines
poisoning the water bed with fertilizer toxins
replaced the muscles and the enriched manure of oxen.
We don't have to ruin the earth to produce food.
Krishna Himself demonstrates how to.
By living a simple, small-scale, agricultural life.
Non-capitalistic, non-exploitative farming is the way to thrive.
Plenty of jobs to employ, farming is a lot of labor.
Necessities taken care of, farming is our savior.
Exchange work for food and lodging.
Everybody comfortably sleeps, nobody is starving.
Treat the cow with affection instead of with abuse and fear.
Like humanity has done before, with love, for thousands of years.
The cow won't produce milk in stressful or tense conditions.
So we need to be on our best behavior to acquire her nutrition.
But factory farms bypass her hormones and suck it out.
Save the cow! Protect her now!

Twelve

Cow's milk develops finer brain tissues for spiritual understanding.
Grasping the intricacies of transcendental knowledge,
consciousness begins expanding.
Eventually a vegan will be depleted of b-12 and soon will need it.
Without b-12, low red blood cells, weakness, and ill mental health.
Milk has all the necessary vitamins to sustain
human physiological conditions,
but cold milk loses its potency and causes malnutrition.
Hot milk clears up mucus and calms the nerves.
Arthritis and mucus are caused by cold milk, do not serve.
Raw milk is where its at!
But now banned because a few big farmers fed cows crap.
Whiskey distillery waste toxic hot slop
gave cows disease and poisoned milk, consumer onslaught.
No fear, pasteurization is here!
Pasteurized milk causes lactose intolerance.
Kills the enzyme lactase needed to digest all of it.
Extreme heat kills all in the milk and the milk itself.
Dead milk profits, but has no benefit to our health.

Thirteen

Hammered on the head, concussion guns.
Electric shock, they must be stunned.
Some left conscious by the ankle, hung
upside down, screaming loud, ear to ear,
slit throat, gurgle sounds.
Skinned, severed, dismembered alive.
Only the disconnected couldn't feel their suffering cries.
If you want to see a glimpse of the meat industry,
watch the four minute video, "10 Billion Lives,"
if it's truth you seek.
We need to find cow milk and cheese, pasture-raised with love,
locally, if possible, not for profit commercially.
At least the best we can find and offer it up respectively.

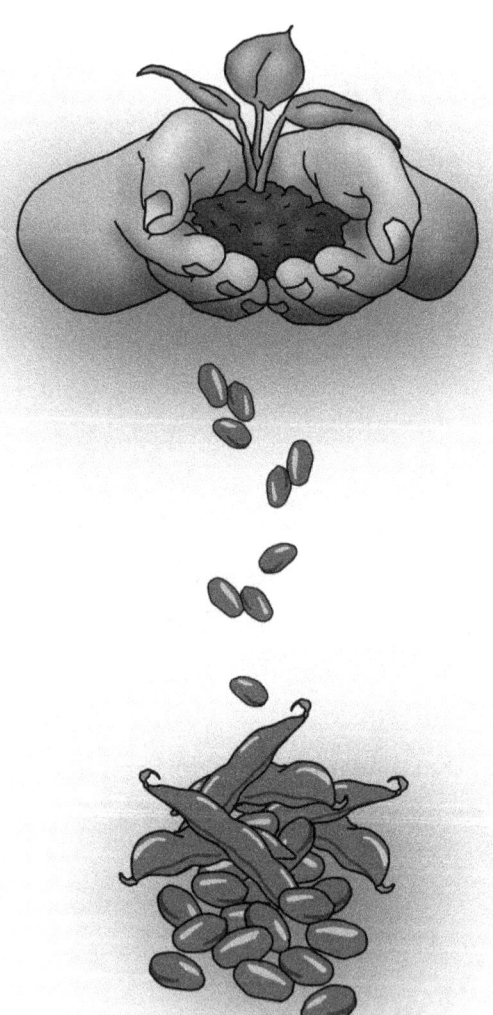

Fourteen

"I have given you every seed yielding plant
that is on the surface of all the earth."
Instructions from God given to our human form of birth.
"And every tree which has fruit yielding seed, it shall be for you."
No flesh in the beginning of Genesis, God says,
"To every beast of the earth, to every fowl of the air,
to every thing that creepeth upon the earth where in there, is life,
I have given every green herb for meat," and it was so...
But man denied and caused strife.
The original Greek word translated as "meat" is phago,
which simply means "to eat."
Here we clearly see, "But flesh with the life thereof
which is the blood thereof, shall ye not eat."
We have dominion over life. A God conscious man knows
that means we provide protection for all that is alive.
"Thou shall not kill."
Men distort this law so they don't feel any guilt.
Can kill animals, but don't kill man.
Don't you think he had the intelligence
to use the right word for us to comprehend? Kill.
We cheat ourselves and others rather than listen to Him.
Spiritually Ill.

Fifteen

Animal killing violates the law of karma.
Simply eating the meat associates us with the slaughter.
"As you sow, so shall you reap."
"Do unto others as you would have them do unto you."
"Treat others how you want to be treated."
"With every action there is an equal and opposite reaction."
When we cause harm or violence to other living beings,
in return, we must experience equivalent suffering.
Either now or later, birth after birth.
It's how the universe stays balanced,
but we can break the curse.
First, it must be addressed that killing plants is still violence.
But there is a vast difference between
killing an animal and harvesting collard greens.
Less pain felt for plants,
their consciousness is not quite as advanced.

Sixteen

Here's how we get out of the curse.
Lord Krishna says
eat only vegetarian foods, but offer it to Him first
with gratitude, love, and in sacrifice. He protects us
from the karma of our past and this life.
Prasadam, sanctified food, means God's mercy.
"'If One offers me with love and devotion
a leaf, a flower, fruit or water, I will accept it.'
Purport: 'We should understand that he will not accept
meat, fish, and eggs.
Vegetables, grains, fruits, milk, and water
are the proper foods for human beings,
and are prescribed by Lord Krishna Himself.'"
-Bhagavad Gita 9.27
The Sanskrit word toyam means "fluid."
In this category water and milk are included.
The word yoga means "union" or "link," meaning
to get in touch with the supreme Lord, offering
food to Him. Yoga, in it's highest form.
Any system of yoga is an attempt to reconnect
our broken relationship with the supreme
personality of Godhead.
Bhakti yoga is the best, it's direct,
our loving relationship with God develops
and we connect.

Seventeen

This human form of life
gives us a chance to know Him.
By devotional service we can go back home again.
We can only understand God by devotional service,
or bhakti,
then we understand ourselves and know our purpose.
The summary of bhakti, the Lord says,
"All that you do, all that you eat, and all that you offer
and give away, as well as all austerites
that you may perform, should be done as an offering,
unto me".
-*Bhagavad Gita 9.27*

References

ISCOWP.org (International Society for Cow Protection)
Click on "Education", then click "What is cow protection?"
By Madhava Priya dasi.
- Dung is a gold mine - Cow and oxen protection

Cows and cow protection Krishna.com
By Hare Krishna Devi Dasi, Hare Krishna Dasi, Sureswara Dasa, and Lavangalatika Devi Dasi.

Why Pasteurized Milk is Bad for Your Health
By Ty Bollinger

1vigor.com/article/raw-milk-nutrient-content
By Ralph Teller

Yoga International.com/Ayurvedic Dairy: The Raw Story of Milk, Yogurt and More. *By David Frawley*

The Book The Higher Taste
By Bhutatma Dasa (Austin Gordon, PhD), Kurma Dasa, Drutakarma Dasa (Michael A. Cremo), & Mukunda Goswami

www.ingramcontent.com/pod-product-compliance
Lightning Source LLC
Chambersburg PA
CBHW031507040426
42444CB00007B/1242